Pepper and Daisy's Adventure

By Annie Richardson

Produced and Manufactured by Softwood Books

EU Responsible person: Maddy Glenn
Office 2, Wharfside House, Prentice Road, Stowmarket, Suffolk, IP14 1RD
www.softwoodbooks.com, hello@softwoodbooks.com

EU Rep:
Authorised Rep Compliance Ltd., Ground Floor, 71 Lower Baggot Street, Dublin, D02 P593, Ireland
www.arccompliance.com, info@arccompliance.com

A CIP catalogue record for this book is available from the British Library

Paperback ISBN: 978-1-0683980-4-9
Hardback ISBN: 978-1-0683980-0-1

"Such a lovely, well written story about the two bunnies who decided to go on an adventure whilst the village are all out looking for them. You are gripped from the beginning. The pictures within the book really help your imagination go wild.

I would recommend this book to all readers especially grandparents whom may have been in a similar situation. I can't wait to hear more about what Pepper and Daisy get up to the next time they visit."

– Jess Ellis

Daisy and Pepper were sad they were having to leave their lovely home where they were able to hop around the garden all day long.

Esmeralda was going on a long summer holiday with her mummy travelling in France in their campervan.

Esmeralda had given **Daisy** her name as she was pure white with a bright yellow nose, which made her think of the pretty daisy flower in her garden, and **Pepper** because he was black and grey, just like pepper.

Daisy and Pepper were going to stay at Esmeralda's grandma and grandpa's house. They did not have a secure garden to run around in like they did at home, but her grandparents had made them a special house and run to play and scamp around.

They would feed them special treats of strawberry and raspberry leaves from their garden.

Esmeralda waved Daisy and Pepper off with a little tear in her eye. She was sad to be leaving them but was happy to be spending her holidays away with her mummy.

"See you in three weeks," said Esmeralda. "Be good for Grandma and Grandpa."

Pepper and Daisy settled in Esmeralda's grandparents' garden. They had lots of fresh water and snacks of broccoli leaves, courgette flowers, and seeds, and they settled down for the night.

The next day, Pepper asked Daisy if she would like to go on a little adventure.

"Shall we try and escape and go on an adventure?" said Pepper.

"You know you are so clever at burrowing," said Pepper to Daisy.

"OK," said Daisy. "It could be fun."

Daisy had spent most of the night burrowing a large hole in the garden and at last the hole was big enough to get through.

"Come on, let's go before we are seen," said Pepper.

They hopped out of the hole and down to the end of the garden where they saw a gap between the fence.

"Come on," said Pepper, we can get out through here!" And off they went to explore!

Grandpa would get up and check on Daisy and Pepper early each morning, but on the second morning they were nowhere to be seen.

"Oh No!" shouted Grandpa! "The Rabbits have escaped!"

Grandma came rushing down the stairs.

"Oh No!"

"What shall we do?"

"We must go and search for them!" said Grandma.

"But they could be anywhere!" said Grandpa.

"We must find them," said Grandma. "Esmeralda will never let us look after them again!"

Grandma and Grandpa lived near a railway line. They alerted the village, sent a neighbourhood message out and stopped everyone on their way to work. Grandpa searched outside near the house, then Grandma had a funny feeling in her tummy.

"Oh No, What if they had decided to try and run home and had managed to get to the platform at the train station."

Grandma ran as fast as she could to the train station.

There were lots of people waiting for the train.

"Has anyone seen a black or white rabbit?" She asked.

"Yes," said one of the people waiting, "I have seen a black rabbit, it was down at the other end of the platform." Grandma thanked the lady and went as fast as she could, and there sitting right near the edge of the platform was Pepper.

"Oh, Pepper," said Grandma, "we have been so worried! We thought we had lost you forever." She gently picked him up, gave him lots of hugs and kisses, and went to find Grandpa.

Grandpa secured the hole where Pepper and Daisy had escaped, and Grandma popped him back with a large broccoli stalk, his favourite vegetable, whilst they went to find Daisy.

Grandma and Grandpa spent all morning searching everywhere. They were beginning to think they would never see Daisy again!

Then, late the same afternoon, their neighbour called Jess rang Grandma.

"Someone in the village had spotted Daisy on the Railway Line near the house," she said.

"You need to go right now; a train is due to come in seven minutes."

Grandma shouted for Grandpa, and they both went running up to the station.

The Station Lady, however, would not let them venture onto the line. "You cannot go down there. It is too dangerous. **Stop! Look! Listen!** You need to alert the Signal Man and wait for him to let you go onto the line."

"Oh no," shouted Grandma. "I can see Daisy. Look! She is right by the track!"

"Oh no," shouted Grandpa. "THE TRAIN!"

And with that, Grandma had her hand over her eyes as the train came towards Daisy.

"I can't look!" said Grandma as the train came into the station. After the train had left the station, Grandma looked up and there she and Grandpa could still see Daisy, she was munching on some leaves.

As soon as Grandma and Grandpa had permission from the Station Master, Grandpa was off! He ran as fast as he could until he got near to Daisy then slowed down, spoke to her quietly and picked her up.

"Phew," said Grandma and Grandpa. "That was close!"

At the end of Peppers and Daisy's adventures, Daisy and Pepper snuggled up to each other and dreamt of their adventures, all the animal friends they had talked to while hopping about, the tortoise, the frog and the little robin, as well as the delicious things they had found to munch on.

"Good night," said Daisy to Pepper.

"Good night, Daisy. It was fun, wasn't it?"

After that, Grandma and Grandpa were on rabbit watch day and night, and never ever did they again let them out of their sight until they were able to take them back home!

Do you think Grandma and Grandpa told Esmeralda how they had nearly lost her Rabbits?

This is my first children's book, based on true events when our granddaughter left her lop-eared bunnies over the summer holidays of 2023. The story is about two very naughty rabbits who escaped whilst in our care.

I would like to thank Niki and Matthew for their support, our daughter Katie, my friends for their encouragement, and my publisher for making this happen.

This book is dedicated to my granddaughter.

Other titles by the same author:

Grandpa's Reindeer (2025)

Pepper & Daisy's Winter Adventure (2026)